THiS BOOK BELONGS TO:

Dedicated to my
loving husband, Marty.

Written by Joan Pearce.
Cover design and illustrations
by Rebekah Phillips Zendzian.

Channel of Love Ministries
http://www.joanpearce.org
PO Box 20069, Bradenton, FL 34204

ISBN: 978-1-958404-49-2 (hardback)

The Good Shepherd

BY JOAN PEARCE

Channel of Love Ministries

David was a young shepherd boy who watched over his father's sheep.

He also loved to worship God.

God saw David's heart, and God sees your heart, too!

David was a good shepherd who carefully watched over his sheep.

Once, a lion and a bear tried to attack the flock, and God gave David enough strength to defend the sheep and save them!

A man of God named Samuel was told to choose a new king for Israel.

He went to David's dad and asked to speak to all of his sons. The man of God said, "None of these young men are the chosen king. Do you have another child?"

"Yes, there's one more, but he's just a young boy!" David's dad said.

"Call for him at once!" Samuel replied.

David's dad called for him to come home from watching over the sheep, and Samuel chose David to be the future king!

God chose a child! A child just like you! What do you think God has planned for your life?

Will you let Him direct your path?

1 Samuel 16:7 "...People judge by the outward appearance, but the Lord looks at the heart."

War broke out in Israel, and David was told to take lunch to his older brothers on the battlefield.

There, on the battlefield, was a giant making fun of God and God's people.

The entire army was afraid of the giant, but David was not afraid because he remembered how God had given him strength to overcome the bear and the lion.

He swung his sling at the giant, and
the giant fell! God's people won
the war!

You don't ever need to be afraid when
big challenges come your way.
God is always going to be with you
to give you strength.

Young David gained favor with the king of Israel after he defeated the giant, but King Saul had an evil spirit that tormented his mind.

The only thing that would bring the king peace was when David played his harp.

But then, King Saul began to get JEALOUS...

and he turned on David.

Do you ever find yourself getting jealous
of your brother, sister, or friend?
This does not please God.

We need to love one another and realize that we don't need to be jealous because God has a special plan for each of us.

When David turned thirty years old, he was crowned the new king of Israel.

King David brought God's ark (which carried God's presence) into town ahead of a parade. He was so excited that he danced passionately as he worshiped God. Some of the people made fun of him because of the way he danced.

You don't ever need to be afraid of being different from other children. God sees your worth even when others don't.

David made some BIG mistakes as king, which made him really sad. When you do things wrong and feel really upset, the enemy will sometimes try to tell you that God is too mad at you and that He won't accept you.

Remember, the enemy doesn't tell the truth. God will never reject you. He loves you and will always be there for you!

Be like David. He went to God and said, "Please, forgive me?" And God forgave him. God will forgive you, too!

Jesus is OUR king and good shepherd.

You are His little lamb.

Jesus loves all
the children of
the world.

God loves you so much that He sent Jesus to die on the cross to forgive you of all your sins.

John 3:16 *For God so loved the world that he gave his one and only Son, that whoever believes in him shall not perish but have eternal life.*

He made a way for you to have eternal life.

God wants you to go to Heaven. Open your heart and ask Jesus to come into your heart. Let's pray together:

Dear Jesus,

I ask you to forgive me for all the bad things that I've done in my life. I ask Jesus to come into my heart and take control of my life. Father in Heaven, please fill me with your Holy Spirit, and help me to live my life like Jesus. I want to do what's right. Thank you, Jesus, for loving me and for being my good shepherd.

LET'S ANSWER SOME QUESTIONS!

1. When you read the last page of the book, did you take the time to say the prayer?

_____

2. What are some of the things you can do to get closer to God?

_____

_____

3. What do you think God has planned for your life?

_____

4. God loves you so much! Do you feel Jesus' love in your heart? What are some of the ways in which you can show God's love to others?

_____

 THE NAME OF MY CHURCH IS:

ON THIS DATE, I ASKED JESUS INTO
 MY HEART!

ON THIS DATE, I WAS BAPTIZED!

MY FAVORITE BIBLE VERSE IS:

WHY I WROTE THIS STORY:

I was raised without a father. All I wanted my entire life was to have a daddy who would buy me ice-cream and take me places. When I was seven years old, my mother remarried, and I remember being so excited because I finally had a papa! But shortly after the marriage, it wasn't what I had hoped for, and my stepfather was very mean to me. My little heart was filled with anger and rage. This caused me to be lonely and have trouble in school. I used to cry a lot. As I got older, I didn't trust people, especially men, and I was very mad at God, until a neighbor started telling me about Jesus. She wouldn't give up on me. I asked Jesus into my heart, and He filled my heart with His love. And He will do the same for you!